Nineteenth Century America

THE
HOSPITALS

NEW YORK HOSPITAL ABOUT 1807

Nineteenth Century America

THE
HOSPITALS

written and illustrated by
LEONARD EVERETT FISHER

Holiday House · New York

Library of Congress Cataloging in Publication Data

Fisher, Leonard Everett.
  The hospitals.

  (Nineteenth century America)
  Includes index.
  SUMMARY: Traces the history of hospitals in the
United States from the early pesthouses built to
isolate the diseased from the rest of the population
to the development of steadily improving institutions
for the treatment of the sick during the 19th century.
  1. Hospitals—United States—History—19th century
—Juvenile literature. [1. Hospitals—History]
I. Title. II. Series.
RA981.A2F57   362.1′1′0973   79-22357
ISBN 0-8234-0405-6

List of Illustrations

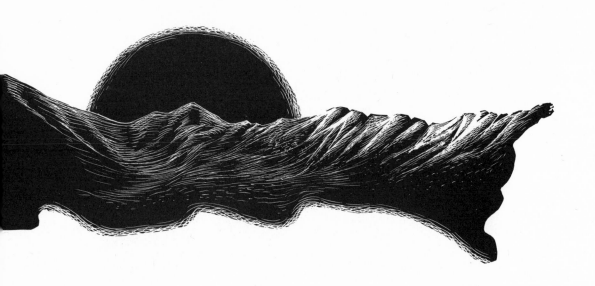

I. 1800-1850

IN 1810, the sun rose over seventeen sovereign states, one district and seven territories* all comprising the very young United States of America. There, in a vast area covering most of the land mass east of the Rocky Mountains from the Canadian border to the Gulf of Mexico, 7,239,881 people† faced the vagaries of New World national life with continuing courage, vitality,

---

*states: Connecticut, Delaware, Georgia, Kentucky, Maryland, Massachusetts, New Hampshire, New Jersey, New York, North Carolina, Ohio, Pennsylvania, Rhode Island, South Carolina, Tennessee, Vermont, Virginia

district: Columbia

territories: Louisiana (covering all or part of present-day Arkansas, Colorado, Iowa, Kansas, Louisiana, Minnesota, Missouri, Montana, Nebraska, North Dakota, Oklahoma, South Dakota, Wyoming); Indiana, Illinois, Michigan, Minnesota, Mississippi, Wisconsin

†United States Government Census, 1810

and optimism. In that year, Americans celebrated their 34th year of independence with hardly a sidelong glance at the first decade of the 19th century through which they had just passed.

The 18th century vanished with George Washington. The first President, having been bled (a common, age-old medical practice) beyond endurance for a sore throat, died December 14, 1799. During that first decade, America sent a naval force to the Mediterranean port of Tripoli, Libya, to punish the Barbary pirates; purchased the Louisiana Territory from France; sent Meriwether Lewis and William Clark off to explore the northwest region; elected Thomas Jefferson and James Madison to the Presidency; mourned the death of former Treasury Secretary Alexander Hamilton, murdered in a duel by former Vice President Aaron Burr; acquitted Burr on a treason charge stemming from his alleged attempt to seize the City of New Orleans with his own army; cheered Robert Fulton's steamboat, *Clermont,* the first of its kind, as it chugged up the Hudson River; cheered again when John Stevens' *Phoenix,* the first ocean-going steamboat, went all the way from New York to Philadelphia; and knew little or nothing at all of a smallpox epidemic raging in Spanish Texas where, in October, 1805, the *Alamo,* a Catholic church and mon-astery in San Antonio, was converted into an isolation hospital for infected military personnel.

America, still a near wilderness but showing signs that

two hundred years of restlessness was creating an ever-widening civilization, was not the most agreeable place for the weak, the destitute, the hesitant, the sick, or the maimed to live in. In that respect, the country was not very different from the rest of the world.

To survive in the overcrowded and unsanitary port cities, or the sometimes-hostile environments of forests, swamps, mountains, and plains, individuals had to be fit and healthy to resist the sure death that was the hand-maiden of badly treated injuries. There were also arrow, knife and gunshot wounds, and contagious diseases that plagued and reduced the population from time to time.

Considering the devastating epidemics of yellow fever, cholera, smallpox, influenza, typhoid fever, and the like that swept across the land at frequent and unexpected intervals, most people continued to view their personal survival with more confidence and enthusiasm than was their due. Town governments did their part in the interest of public health by separating those afflicted with contagious or mysterious diseases from the unafflicted.

"Pesthouses" were built in remote areas to isolate those thought to be contaminated with menacing diseases from the general population. Boston, Massachusetts, designated two areas for the construction of pesthouses early in the 18th century. Both were in the harbor—Deer Island for infected citizens and Spectacle Island for sick immigrants. A pesthouse existed on New York Harbor's Bedloe's Island (now called Liberty

Island) as early as 1738. A single city employee—a common "labourer"—managed and maintained the place. By the beginning of the 19th century, most American port cities, such as Philadelphia, Pennsylvania and Charleston, South Carolina, had their harbor pesthouses as well.

These institutions were not hospitals by even the most minimal standards, however much they served the public health interest. No physicians were in regular attendance at the pesthouses. People committed to such places were not subjected to a curative program of medical care. Pesthouses were unsanitary, unkempt,

PESTHOUSE RESIDENTS

dreary, and dreadful isolation structures in which few survived.

From the dim beginning of recorded time until the first years of the 19th century, institutions existed the world over to house and care for the homeless, the blind, the crippled, the poor, the sick, and even the tired traveler, the orphan, and the aged. Usually these were charitable institutions, founded and run by religious orders. In time, in Latinized Europe, they would be called "hospitalia" or guest houses. Christian Europe would shorten the term to "hospital" and re-define its purpose as an institution to care for and cure with God's help those who were ailing. Thus it was that the pesthouse

was never viewed as a "hospital," since there was no attempt at patient care or any medical service whatever. Nevertheless, American hospitals, regardless of their well-meaning and humanitarian concerns, were not much better than the pesthouses when it came to patient survival until the 1850s.

For the most part, hospitals in America were dirty, dingy, disease-ridden, and infectious places during the first fifty years of the 19th century. Nearly half the people who had limbs amputated in hospitals died of "hospital gangrene." Worse still, about nine out of every ten people who were surgical patients died during their operations or from infections resulting from the operations. No one knew anything about bacteria, cleanliness, or the use of antiseptics. Surgeons operated in street clothes upon patients strapped to adjustable chairs. Usually, the surgeon washed his hands after surgery, not before. It was no wonder that most people refused to enter a hospital if they had the strength to resist, preferring instead to be treated in their homes if they could afford such private treatment—or not be treated at all, especially by a physician or surgeon. Worse still, operations were the most incredibly painful ordeals. Anesthetics—pain-killing or sleep-inducing drugs—were unknown. Patients endured their agony through liquor-fed or opium-induced stupors, or clamped their jaws over a piece of wood before fainting from either their indescribable distress or plain fright.

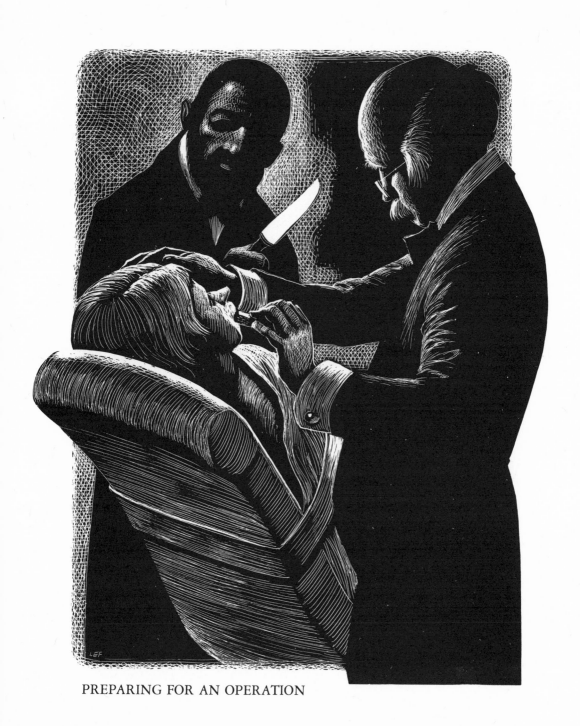

PREPARING FOR AN OPERATION

It was much easier and simpler to put one's faith in Providence. Moreover, there were not enough trained and competent doctors to attend the myriad complaints of a population that would grow from 5,308,483 Americans in 1800 to 23,191,876 Americans in 1850*. What few doctors there were practiced in the densely populated areas and treated the well-to-do. The poor and the not-so-well-to-do went largely unattended by professional medical persons. They relied heavily on prayer and ancestral medical remedies cooked up in the kitchen. Soldiers and sailors were looked after by military doctors.

American merchant seamen fared better than most. In 1798, the Congress enacted a law for the "relief of sick and disabled seamen." The law established the Marine Hospital Service. American national interest was focusing once more on the sea as it did during the Revolutionary War. This time the United States was on the verge of war with France, a former ally, not Britain, a traditional foe. France, nine years past her own bloody revolution, had been raiding American merchant ships looking for goods being shipped to England. America, asserting her belief in freedom of the seas, kept up a running battle with the French navy during 1798-1799, and successfully secured open sea lanes for her ships.

In any case, the United States Government, through

*United States Government Census, 1800 and 1850

the Marine Hospital Service Act of 1798, deducted about twenty cents from the monthly wages of every American able-bodied seaman. This defrayed the cost of treatment at a convenient hospital. Whatever the expense and regardless of how much the seaman paid into the fund, he was entitled to the full measure of the medical services offered. This was the first medical insurance program in the United States. In 1804, the first hospital of the Marine Hospital Service was built in Boston, Massachusetts. By the time the Civil War erupted in 1861, there were thirty such hospitals in American ports serving sick and disabled American seamen. In 1912, the Marine Hospital Service became the United States Public Health Service.

The Marine Hospital Service notwithstanding, there were altogether too few hospitals—as well as competent physicians—to serve the needs of the burgeoning country. Those that did exist were often airless, dark, forbidding, hair-raising establishments that were not soon forgotten by those who managed to survive the experience.

The science of medicine and surgery at the beginning of the 19th century in America as elsewhere, except for a few discoveries and improvements, was still a discipline of timeless ignorance—of hit or miss treatments—of homemade remedies—of your-guess-is-as-good-as-mine curatives.

There was the popular *Dr. Flint's Quaker Bitters,* a

liquid composed of "roots, barks, and herbs." It promised to remove the "infirmities of age," strengthen and stimulate the body, cheer the mind, purify the blood, and produce a vigorous circulation, along with a beautiful and healthy complexion. "No one can remain long unwell (if curable) after taking a few bottles," stated the advertisements of the Dr. H.S.Flint & Co. of Providence, Rhode Island.

Madame Zadoc Porter's Curative Cough Balsam was New York City's answer to coughs, colds, whooping cough, croup, asthma, and "all affections of the Throat and Lunge." Purportedly made of vegetables, this soothing liquid based its curative power of "loosening the phlegm" and "inducing free spitting" on its ability to "assist the healthy and vigorous circulation of the Blood through the Lunge."

One military physician, perplexed by too many cases of Rocky Mountain spotted fever among the troops in Utah late in the century, advised the soldiers not to eat snow. Snow, he reasoned without investigation, contained a natural poisonous element that could kill a human being. The soldiers kept their distance from snow. No one had any idea that the fatal disease was caused by a germ carried by certain wood ticks which injected the germ into the human blood stream with a single bite.

In any event, the first known "hospitall" in British America was founded in 1612 at the "citty of Henricus,"

16

a tiny settlement in the Corporation of Henrico, about eighty miles up the James River from Jamestown, Virginia. This was not the first medical facility in North America, however. That distinction belongs to the Hospital of the Immaculate Conception, established in Mexico City by the Spanish conqueror, Hernando Cortes, sometime between 1524 and 1527. It is still used, although its name was changed to the Hospital of Jesus the Nazarene.

The "hospitall" at Henricus, Virginia, on the other hand, fell into disuse. The colony never lived up to its growth expectations. On March 22, 1622, a near ruinous massacre of the Virginia colony settlers by local Indians under Chief Opechancanough nearly obliterated the English foothold in North America. One of every three or four colonists, men, women and children, were slaughtered. Among the victims were five Henricus colonists, practically all that remained after several years of decline. Nothing further was heard of the "hospitall," and Henricus soon passed into oblivion.

Between 1612 and 1810, during which time the European population in America soared from under a thousand to nearly seven and a half million, only a handful of significant medical establishments were founded in what is now the United States. Not all of these survived the century in which they began, but some went on to become great modern-day medical institutions.

Between 1658 and 1660, the Dutch West India Company of New Amsterdam on the southern tip of Manhattan Island opened a small hospital for its ailing employees in an almshouse, or poorhouse. Almshouses were, more or less, shelters run either by local governments or churches. They provided havens for the homeless blind, the homeless sick, and the homeless poor. Health care had little meaning. A roof overhead and food for the hungry was all that was expected and all that was dispensed. Sometimes, the almshouse residents

DINNER AT AN ALMSHOUSE

did menial labor in exchange for shelter and food. In these instances, the shelter became a "workhouse" to which criminals were committed.

Called the Old Hospital, the New Amsterdam facility was run by a lone matron working under the supervision of the Dutch West India Company physician. In 1664, New Amsterdam became New York. But the Old Hospital continued to grow as it passed from Dutch to English jurisdiction. When the hospital was demolished in 1680, it occupied several made-over workshops of the Dutch West India Company.

Another American hospital with roots in an almshouse was the Philadelphia General Hospital, now the City of Philadelphia Nursing Home. The Philadelphia Almshouse was chartered in 1729 to care for orphans, the destitute, and insane "dependent persons." Over the next 150 years the Philadelphia Almshouse became a sordid, dreaded poorhouse in which orphans, the destitute, the insane, incurably and infectiously ill people, the hopelessly crippled, and numbers of expectant mothers, all intermingled in common wards. The ramshackle group of buildings that contained the almshouse had no lights and no washing facilities, except for one tub. Medical care was irregular. Nursing care was provided by the inhabitants themselves. It was not until the 1880s that a concerted effort was made to end the chaotic conditions.

In 1736, three hospitals were founded in separate

parts of the country: St. Philip's Hospital in Charleston, South Carolina; St. John's Hospital in New Orleans, Louisiana; and the Publick Workhouse and House of Correction of New York City. Only the latter two were destined to survive into the 19th century and become 20th century institutions.

St. Philip's Hospital in Charleston was basically an almshouse. It provided free shelter and nourishment for the city's sick and poor. It also housed criminals. And within its precincts, it extended minor medical care to its "paupers, patients and prisoners." St. Philip's closed its doors in 1789 after 50 years of service.

St. John's Hospital in new Orleans was the gift of a dead sailor who left his fortune for the specific purpose of helping the sick of New Orleans. In the period 1813-1814, following the War of 1812, St. John's Hospital was renamed Charity Hospital. Within ten years it was caring for 120 patients in four sick wards, two fever wards, and one surgical ward. By 1833, Charity Hospital was a 500-bed structure. By mid-20th century, Charity Hospital would become a 3,500-bed general hospital belonging to the people of Louisiana.

Like St. Philip's, The Publick Workhouse and House of Correction of New York City followed the common practice of caring for the sick, the poor, and the incorrigible under one roof—an almshouse, workhouse, and prison combined, with an emphasis on prison-workhouse confinement. Nevertheless, the facility, built on the site of today's City Hall, had its upper floor fitted out in part with a six-bed infirmary for use by any classification of its residents—poor, sick, or prisoner.

For the next sixty-odd years, the building went through a number of changes and enlargements. Finally, the complex was removed to the Kipp's Bay Farm area on the East River at 28th Street. There the city owned parcels of land it had purchased from local farmers between 1794 and 1811. In 1811, several buildings were constructed on a section of the newly acquired land called Belle Vue Place. The group of buildings was called the Belle Vue Establishment. In 1812, the Belle Vue Establishment became a collection center for yellow fever sufferers while still housing the poor, sick, and condemned miscreants of New York. In 1819, further building expansion created more room for additional yellow fever victims, for the newly-admitted insane of New York, for more minor offenders, and for more homeless sick.

Before the first quarter of the 19th century had run its course—the Bellevue Establishment became Bellevue Hospital in 1825—that place had become a hellish nightmare of unsanitary, disorganized, and indifferent care in which two thousand howling, groaning, and weeping souls without hope and in need of some level of medical attention resided. What few nurses there were were tough, medically ignorant women inmates of the prison on Blackwell's Island (now called Roosevelt

21

Island and once known as Welfare Island) in the East River. There was no soap or laundry. Bed linens were no more than filthy rags. There were no dining facilities. Starchy meals were served in the overcrowded wards where the residents ate without benefit of dishes or utensils. They either dug the food out of buckets with bare hands or scooped it up from the raw table planks

A HOSPITAL WARD ABOUT 1830

upon which it had been swilled. Some did not eat at all and died of hunger, not of their ailment.

The conditions at Bellevue were not much different than most nonvoluntary or public, tax-supported hospitals. During the 1830s, the insane wards of the Philadelphia General Hospital were open to public view for common amusement. These social attitudes persisted until the middle of the 19th century, when efforts were made to improve hospital conditions on a wide scale.

Several other noteworthy medical facilities founded in the 18th century grew into the 19th century and beyond.

These were the Philadelphia and New York Dispensaries; and Pennsylvania, New York, and Maryland Hospitals. All were voluntary hospitals—hospitals established by state charter but supported chiefly by private funds rather than by public taxation.

Both the Philadelphia Dispensary, founded in 1786, and the New York Dispensary, founded in 1791, were out-patient institutions. That is, people with an assortment of minor injuries and ailments—ailments that were not contagious and therefore a threat to the health of the general public—were treated on the spot and sent home the same day. There were no facilities in these dispensaries for overnight patients. The Philadelphia and New York Dispensaries were established as charitable institutions to give free out-patient medical care to poor people.

In 1752, the Pennsylvania Hospital opened its doors to both those who could afford to pay and those who could not. Located in Philadelphia and founded by a Marylander, Dr. Thomas Bond, with the aid of Benjamin Franklin, Pennsylvania Hospital was very specific regarding who it would or would not admit. For one thing, the hospital wanted only patients it felt could be cured within a reasonable period of time. "No Patient shall be admitted whose Cases are judged incurable . . .", they said. The only exception made in this regard was "Lunaticks." They did not want to admit individuals suffering with "infectious Distempers" either. Such uncomfortable and dangerous diseases as smallpox were relegated to the isolation of the pesthouse where the victims either died or survived miraculously. Formerly, sick women admitted by a hospital were allowed to bring their children with them, but an end was put to this, and children were no longer permitted to accompany their mothers. The hospital did not want a noisy establishment. Hospital rules made it plain that the deserving poor—those who would work if they were healthy—came first at no charge. Whatever space remained was offered to those who could afford to pay some reasonable rate.

Patients diagnosed as either cured or incurable were discharged from the hospital. Unlike the almshouse, the sick poor, or anyone else in such a place, could not become permanent residents. Moreover, Pennsylvania Hospital patients were forbidden to drink, gamble, swear, or otherwise act crudely. This seems not to have applied to the "keepers" of the insane. The insane, violent or not, were kept in unheated cells. And they were kept, often manhandled, by male keepers of dubious background and qualifications. The physically sick who could, served the others. They did the washing, the cleaning, and the nursing.

Originally occupying a small house on Philadelphia's Market Street, the Pennsylvania Hospital soon moved into a large brick building on the edge of town. There it continued to expand into a more general hospital, while heeding the directive of the Pennsylvania State Assembly to cure "useful and laborious" poor people—the workers—and return them to society.

By the end of the first decade of the 19th century, the

PENNSYLVANIA HOSPITAL, EAST WING, ABOUT 1800

Pennsylvania Hospital was serving the needs of 100 patients a day, more than half of whom were upper-class insane—paying patients. The hospital boasted a 300-seat surgical amphitheater, a medical museum, and a library. By 1825, the hospital was again receiving more poor, nonpaying patients than paying. And by 1850, its medical library was the largest in the United States.

New York Hospital received its charter in 1771 for some of the same reasons that Pennsylvania Hospital was founded: to restore the health of the "industrious and laborious poor among us"—again, the "deserving poor"—and return them to their communities to lead productive lives. Also, the idea of New York Hospital, to be located on lower Broadway, was strongly supported by the medical profession. Physicians Samuel Bard, John Jones, and Peter Middleton, all professors in the medical school at King's College, now Columbia University, reasoned that a hospital would provide opportunities for more practical instruction. Such a connection had already existed between Pennsylvania Hospital and the medical school of the College of Philadelphia, when in 1768, a medical school was founded at Columbia College. In any event, New York Hospital did not receive its first patient until 1791. The American revolution and a disastrous fire were among the chief obstacles to the opening of the hospital during the twenty years following the granting of the charter by the State of New York.

Unlike Pennsylvania Hospital which was maintaining only upperclass paying insane while referring the poor insane to the former Philadelphia Almshouse— the Philadelphia General Hospital—during the period 1800-1820, New York Hospital admitted the insane of any class. These were housed in rooms separate from the rest of the hospital. In 1805, these quarters were found to be "imbued with filth . . . extremely offensive . . . unwholesome." Five years later, these same rooms were deemed to be the best managed in the whole hospital. By that time, 1810, considerable progress had been made at the hospital for the housing of the insane. No longer were they maintained in rooms separated from the hospital's regular wards; they were now housed in a separate building built especially for them.

In addition to promoting better living conditions for the insane, a program fathered by Dr. Benjamin Rush, a signer of the Declaration of Independence and responsible for the insane at Pennsylvania Hospital until his death in 1813, New York Hospital installed the first surgical amphitheatre in America in 1803. Two years before that the first maternity ward was established in New York Hospital.

Maryland Hospital in Baltimore, founded in 1797, was not very much different in its bricked-up appearance, patient care, and attitude than its sister institutions in Pennsylvania and New York. Its patient capacity was about the same as Pennsylvania Hospital —about 100 patients. And like Pennsylvania Hospital

THE INSANE

and New York Hospital, by 1812 it seemed to be preoccupied with the humane housing of the insane in its still incompleted building.

In fact, concern for America's mentally ill led to the establishment of numerous facilities for the care and treatment of the 'insane,' beginning with Eastern State Hospital for the mentally ill in Williamsburg, Virginia, in 1773. Most of these institutions, however, were private or affiliated with hospitals. Where there were no available institutions, those judged insane were sent to almshouses, poorhouses, workhouses, and even jails. Some of the more sensitive institutions, like the Bloomingdale Asylum of New York, attempted as early as 1821 to create a pleasant environment for their mental patients and treat them with kindness. Here the insane were not chained, starved, tortured, drugged, bled, and forgotten, sources of amusement, experiment, or the hapless victims of the medical ignorance of the day.

Between 1825 and midcentury, the public outcry regarding the quality of the hospitalization of the insane was enough to effect some change for the better in their lives. Largely through the crusading efforts of Dorothea L. Dix of Boston, humane state insane asylums were created by state legislatures everywhere during the 1840s. In these institutions, the mentally ill could find some protection from the barbarism to which many had been subjected. The problems and mysteries of mental illness were overwhelming, however. Jammed with

30

more hopeless people than could be managed, the new state hospitals for the insane could not function properly. The overcrowding paralyzed any planned medical treatment program if there was such a program at all. These hospitals became, for the most part, listless halfway houses to nowhere, where no one was brutalized as in the past and where no one was treated for any disorder as they would be one day in the distant future.

Finally, the first major hospital of the modern era without roots in 18th century colonial American medical or charitable institutions was founded in Boston, Massachusetts. In 1811, John Collins Warren, a physician-founder of the Harvard Medical School, thought that in the interest of thorough medicine a hospital should be connected to the medical school. Accordingly, he and another doctor, James Jackson, raised the money from Boston wealth and helped establish Massachusetts General Hospital. It took ten years to raise the money and construct the hospital. In 1821, Massachusetts General Hospital began to serve the "sick and miserable" of Boston.

On October 16, 1846, an event of far-reaching significance occurred at Massachusetts General Hospital that would dramatically improve the course of medicine world-wide as well as the perception of a hospital.

On that day, Gilbert Abbott, a house painter with a tumor on his face, was anesthetized by ether in the operating amphitheatre of the hospital by William

Thomas Green Morton, a 35-year-old-dentist. With six other prominent surgeons in attendance around the patient and an audience of medical students looking on, John Collins Warren, cut the growth from Mr. Abbott's face. The patient felt nothing but a "scraping" of his "neck". There was no pain. "Gentlemen," said Dr. Warren to the audience, "this is no humbug."

This was not the first time ether had been used to dull or eliminate pain in a surgical procedure. Dr. Morton had extracted the tooth of an ether breathing patient in his own office several weeks before. In 1842, Georgia surgeon, Dr. Crawford Long, removed two small tumors from the back of the neck of a Mr. James M. Venables while the patient inhaled ether. There was no pain connected with this operation either. Unfortunately, Dr. Long never reported the incident until later. In any event, the operation that took place at Massachusetts General Hospital marked the first time that ether was used as an anaesthetic in a hospital by a renowned physician in the company of renowned physicians before a general medical audience. Others claimed credit for the discovery: Dr. Charles Thomas Jackson and Dr. Horace Wells—the former a physician, the latter a dentist. Although the controversy raged on for years with a despondent Wells committing suicide, the fact remained that the use of ether at "Mass. General" by Drs. Warren and Morton made surgery more acceptable and the hospital less fearful to the general public.

MORTON

J.C. WARREN

ABBOTT

DR. MORTON ADMINISTERING ETHER

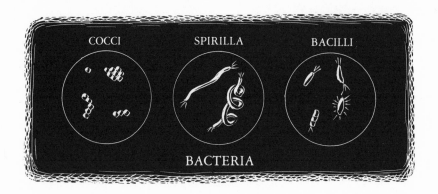

COCCI SPIRILLA BACILLI

BACTERIA

II. 1850-1899

AT MIDCENTURY, the American medical profession stood on the threshold of stunning discoveries that would not only revolutionize the practice of surgery through the use of anesthetics, but would also improve the medical sciences of pathology and physiology—the sciences concerning the nature of diseases and the functions of living organs. Before the century would end, Joseph Lister, an English surgeon, would show that surgical cleanliness through the use of antiseptics—chiefly carbolic acid—to kill death-dealing invisible organisms in open wounds could dramatically reduce infections and the high incidence of surgical deaths. Lister took his cue from the experiments of French scientist, Louis Pasteur, who in the 1850s finally proved what some had long suspected—that bacteria—which could only be seen under a microscope, were without doubt the cause of disease.

By the end of the century, the use of rubber gloves in surgery, first demonstrated by Dr. Joseph C. Bloodgood of Johns Hopkins Hospital in Baltimore, would become almost routine in a general program of complete hospital sterilization to prevent infection.

Also, by the end of the century, German scientist Wilhelm Konrad Roentgen would invent the X ray. At last, doctors would have an immediate diagnostic or investigative tool that would end much medical guesswork by unraveling some of the heretofore unseen mysteries of the living body.

Altogether, anesthetics, antiseptics, sterilization, and X ray held the promise of a higher health standard, a better recovery rate, and a longer more productive life for all. The change and the challenge was in the wind. While there were those who would resist the new knowledge, there were those with enough vision, daring, and intelligence to embark on these uncharted medical courses. The American hospital stood poised and ready to deal with new ideas.

Until the end of the first quarter of the 19th century, only four structures in America had been designed and built strictly as hospitals—as places devoted solely to caring for the sick. These were Philadelphia's Pennsylvania Hospital, New York Hospital in New York City, Charity Hospital in New Orleans, and Boston's Massachusetts General Hospital.

The other medical institutions either occupied structures not originally designed as hospitals or else built structures that included hospitals as elements of other services. The latter would include poorhouses, almshouses, workhouses and jails. All of these facilities except one were charitable places supported by private funds. Only Bellevue Hospital in New York was supported by the public— a situtation that would begin to change toward the end of the 19th century when more and more hospital construction and support was funded by public tax dollars.

Also, until the 1850s, the traditon of freely hospitalizing first the insane, then the contagious, followed by the poor with various infectious maladies, was a matter of unquestioned routine. Few considered privacy essential for those whose minds were out of focus and disoriented—the insane or mentally disturbed; for the contagious whose frightful symptoms required banishment and isolation from the public; and for the poor, whose lives began and ended in crowded squalor anyway. The wealthy, of course, were rarely publicly hospitalized other than those who were mentally ill or infected with a contagious disease. Ordinary sickness and injury of the well-to-do was treated at home.

Until the middle of the 19th century, hospital planning did little for the privacy of the patient. And the conditions within the confines of these hospitals were, for the most part, so frightful as to send those who thought they were sick into hiding and give shudders to the rest. There were no private rooms to speak of—at least not until the end of the century when charitably motivated hospitals gave way to paying, voluntary hospitals. At that point, those who could afford to pay for whatever hospital service they required were more readily admitted to hospitals than those who could not pay. Some of those admitted demanded more private accommodations. Private rooms became commonplace for those who could afford them. And these rooms together with their occupants and visitors took on more of an aspect of hotel than hospital.

In any case, the lack of privacy was in part due to the lack of hallways. The so-called "block" plan of hospital design permitted passage through the building, from one section to another, only through the crowded wards. Sometimes curtained cubicles were arranged in these wards to effect a modicum of privacy. Men and women were maintained in separate wards.

Regardless, the sick inhabitants of these common wards which rarely made distinctions between race, religion, creed, or ethnic background, had no protection from the constant stream of noisy traffic that went by. Moreover, the design inherent in the block plan was so compact that no sunshine, daylight or fresh air could penetrate the spaces.

Florence Nightingale, an English nurse, believed that sunshine—or at least some daylight—and fresh air were elements essential to good health and to the

37

recovery of the sick. She advocated the idea that hospital wards need not be dark, dingy, smelly walkthroughs. She insisted that each ward be a separate wing of a building with windows all around except at the one end where each of the wards would be connected to a common corridor. The design, which had roots in medieval Europe, was called the "pavilion" plan. It made use of long, narrow, finger-like buildings—appendages—connected at one end to a hall.

The first hospital in the United States to incorporate the pavilion plan was Philadelphia's Presbyterian Hospital. Founded in 1860 as America moved inexorably

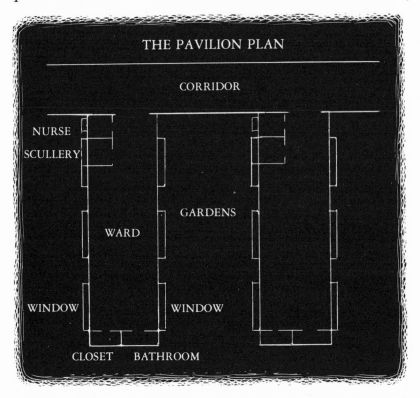

toward civil war, Presbyterian was not, however, the first American hospital to separate hospital traffic from the sick ward. In 1854, St. Luke's Hospital in New York City did just that with a design that included corridors running parallel to and alongside the wards. While this arrangement removed unwanted traffic from the wards, it did not improve the problems of poor ventilation and little light.

The usefulness of the pavilion plan as demonstrated by Presbyterian Hospital in Philadelphia was an immediate success. Nearly every hospital built in the United States over the next fifty or sixty years, such as the Rhode Island Hospital in Providence or New York's Roosevelt Hospital, both erected in the 1860s, was based on the pavilion plan.

Another group of American "firsts" that had more to do with people than with buildings were the events dealing with the beginnings of the New York Infirmary for Women and Children.

English-born Elizabeth Blackwell received her medical degree in 1849 from the Geneva Medical School of New York. Dr. Blackwell's achievement was astonishing at the time. She had become the first woman in the world to be legally admitted to the practice of medicine, and thus entered a profession that had been the private domain of men since the beginning. Two other women quickly joined their colleague: Emily Blackwell, her sister, and Marie Zakrzewska, a friend. Both of these women received their medical degrees from Cleveland Medical College in Cleveland, Ohio.

An irrepressible advocate of women's rights during the women's movements of the 1840s and 1850s, Elizabeth Blackwell, M.D. was forced to continue her medical education in Europe because no American hospital would accept her for advanced training. Even upon her return to the United States, she was prevented from seeing patients in hospitals.

Undaunted, Dr. Blackwell, together with her sister and Dr. Marie Zakrzewska, established the New York Infirmary for Women and Children—a hospital for

DR. ELIZABETH BLACKWELL

women and their offspring run by women. That happened in 1853. No other such hospital had ever existed before. Fifteen years later, in 1868, the three women physicians established another medical institution, the Women's Medical College—a bona fide medical school which admitted qualified women only. No such medical school had ever existed before.

Despite fierce opposition from the vast majority of American doctors, Drs. Blackwell and Zakrzewska established a precedent with their special hospital and medical school. They received enough encouragement to finally open the doors of the medical profession to more and more qualified women.

The apparent success and medical usefulness of the New York Infirmary for Women and Children quickly led to the founding of another similar hospital devoted to the medical problems of women.

In 1855, two years after Elizabeth Blackwell and her colleagues opened their infirmary, Dr. James Marion Sims founded the Women's Hospital of the State of New York, also called the New York State Hospital for Women. Sims, a southerner by birth, came to New York at the age of 40, an ailing but already renowned surgeon, obstetrician and gynecologist—a specialist in women's diseases. He had been practicing in Alabama and felt uncomfortable in the southern climate. Dr. Sims' New York State Hospital for Women became the heart of gynecological medicine and surgery in the United States, and he is regarded today as the father of modern gynecology.

Sims' success was an intriguing personal achievement. In his autobiography, *The Story of My Life,* published in New York in 1889, six years after his death, he described his politician, tavern-owning father's opposition to the medical profession and his own choice of a medical career:

". . . I cannot control you," Sims recalls his father saying. ". . . It is a profession for which I have the utmost contempt. There is no science in it. There is no honor to be achieved in it; no reputation to be made, and to think that my son should be going around from house to house through the country, with a box of pills in one hand and a squirt [syringe] in the other, to ameliorate human suffering, is a thought I never supposed I should have to contemplate."

Whether or not the elder Sims expressed his distaste for his son's profession in such exactly remembered language is, perhaps, a matter of Dr. Sims' literary style. Nevertheless, the conservative attitude and general mistrust implicit in the statement is a significant indication of the level of esteem in which doctors and hospitals were held during the early 19th century and for a long time thereafter.

Having ignored his father's indifference to human suffering, Dr. Sims went on to complete a world-wide, illustrious career by suggesting the idea of a special hospital for the treatment of cancer. Shortly before his death in 1883, the 70-year-old Sims proposed that funds be raised to build a center for the treatment and perhaps the study of cancer. The concept developed in the drawing rooms of New York society, largely because one of New York's prominent families had a history of cancer fatalities.

DR. JAMES MARION SIMS

Sims died, but his idea lived. In 1884, the New York Cancer Hospital—today's Memorial Hospital—was born with funds contributed by New York City's philanthropic wealthy: the Astors, the Vanderbilts, and the Morgans, among others.

The Vanderbilts continued to be active in the support of New York medical institutions. Four years after the New York Cancer-Memorial Hospital became a reality the Vanderbilts contributed the Vanderbilt Clinic to Columbia University and the poor of New York. The clinic was a dispensary serving the ailing poor of the city on an out-patient basis only. The medical care that was given at no charge to the patients was provided by the faculty of Columbia Medical College, their staff, and the students themselves.

During the period of the Civil War, 1861-1865, both sides in the conflict, North and South, established networks of hospitals to care for the sick and wounded. In 1862, the surgeon general of the Union Army, Dr. William A. Hammond, established hospitals for non-battle-connected diseases being suffered by soldiers in the ranks. One such hospital was located in Philadelphia. The effort began a trend toward specialized medicine and surgery that gained momentum after the war. Enough records were kept by both sides indicating that more soldiers died of disease than of wounds inflicted in battle. Of the approximately 3,500,000 men in uniform, 160,000 died of wounds while 375,000 died of sickness.

Field hospitals were often large complexes of tents serving both the sick and the wounded. Every army brigade, division, and corps set up a field hospital with full surgical service, if they were bivouacked in an area for any length of time.

During the winter of 1863-1864, the Second Army Corps (Union) established a large field hospital in the woods at Brandy Station on the Orange & Alexandria Railroad in Virginia. Brandy Station, north of Culpepper and not far from Washington, D.C., was the site of the bloodiest cavalry battle in the Civil War, June 9, 1863. The battle was the prelude for Gettysburg a month later. The field hospital, however, was filled up with soldiers who had contracted diseases while in the ranks.

The field hospital was virtually a tent city. Each tent had a wood floor to protect its occupants from the damp earth. And each tent had a wood burning stove that was tended to day and night. According to Alexander Gardner, a military photographer who worked for Matthew Brady, whose job it was to photograph the Civil War, "blankets were furnished in the greatest abundance, and every attention was shown the patients by experienced surgeons."

Like most military field hospitals of the Civil War, the Second Corps hospital was visited by the various sanitary commissions from the town, city, or state whose purpose was to watch over the sick and wounded

45

sons of their particular districts, to protect their health interests, and to see to it that these soldiers received bed linens, home cooked food, books, magazines, and newspapers. The more national Christian Commission not only provided the same compassionate service but included religious comfort as well.

Alexander Gardner also wrote, "There was a brotherhood among the patients . . . Those who endured the

AN ARMY HOSPITAL

sufferings of the Camp Hospital . . . learned to care for each other's welfare, and many now look back to the weary days of hospital life as the beginnings of friendship which time cannot weaken or adversity estrange."

The end of the Civil War not only brought progress in medicine and surgery—new treatments, more research, and radical surgical procedures performed under the pressure of battle—but a renewal and expansion of the American spirit.

While thousands of hopefuls had flocked to California

during the 1850s after gold was discovered at Sutter's Mill in 1849, the real thrust westward did not occur until after the war was over and the transcontinental railroad was completed in 1869. According to the United States Census Bureau, the American frontier ceased to be a frontier twenty-four years later in 1893. Alaska, Arizona, Hawaii, New Mexico, Oklahoma, and Utah were not yet states of the Union, however. And the American frontier, although well on the road to orderly civilization, was as disorderly, rowdy, and dangerous as Hudson River farms were orderly, calm, and peaceful.

The life of the westward moving pioneer, or the prospector, cowboy, and storekeeper west of the Mississippi River was as unpredictable as a Kansas tornado. There were numerous physicians and surgeons—or those who called themselves doctors—out West who dug out bullets from gunshot wounds with unwashed, ungloved fingers; amputated limbs without benefit of anything more antiseptic than a bottle of whiskey; operated on men, women, and children without so much as removing their hats, dressed in street clothes protected by blood encrusted aprons; sewed up wounds with catgut pinned to the lapels of their coats; and once in a while, in difficult cases, delivered babies whose mothers would have marveled about the likes of the New York Infirmary for Women and Children or the New York State Hospital for Women had they heard of either

PREPARING TO REMOVE
A BULLET IN THE WEST

institution. The plain fact was that the doctor on the American frontier—in the mines or mining towns, farms or ranches—worked in shacks, kitchens, cabins, barns, saloons, tents, and in the open air without benefit of the sophisticated hospitals that dotted the East. At the end of the Civil War, there were only 200 hospitals in the United States and about 80 of these were scat-

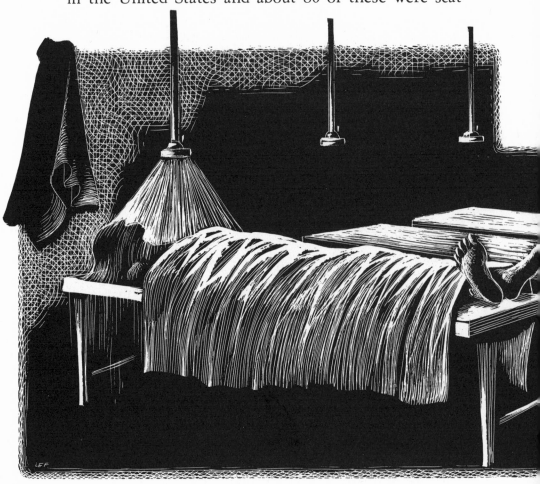

THE BELLEVUE MORGUE

tered between New York and Pennsylvania.

Immediately following the close of the Civil War, various medical services were initiated by hospitals not only to improve patient care, but also to reach out to people in need beyond the hospital ward. In 1866, the City of New York built the first American modern morgue at Bellevue Hospital. Too many people were dying and being buried in Potter's Field before proper identification of the deceased could be established. The morgue was a cold, stone-walled room with a water

sprinkler system that sprayed the corpses for preservation until some relative or friend answered a newspaper advertisement and made the identification.

Three years later, in 1869, Bellevue Hospital installed the country's first ambulance service. While the Union Army did have a horse-drawn ambulance detail on occasion during the war, no private or public hospital supported such a service until the Bellevue innovation. It was called the New York Ambulance Service. By 1884, five hospitals in New York City had an ambulance service: Bellevue, New York, Presbyterian, St. Vincent's and Roosevelt. Like the Fire Department, the ambulance service was on call twenty-four hours a day, seven

AN AMBULANCE

days a week. All of the ambulances were horse-drawn, enclosed wagons. And each of them had a loud brass bell. The ambulance had the right of way over all traffic except fire engines and the wagons of the post office. Strangely, it seemed more important at the time to have the mail delivered promptly than it was to deliver a suffering human being to a hospital and perhaps save a life.

In 1873, following the beginning of ambulance service, three major hospitals established schools of nursing: Bellevue in New York, Boston's Massachusetts General, and New Haven Hospital in New Haven, Connecticut. Until the middle of the 19th century, and for centuries before, nursing was the province of religious orders. Some of these orders like the Catholic Sisters of Charity were specifically established as nursing orders. If nursing nuns were unavailable, then nursing was left either to the patients themselves helping one another or to the incompetent aid of illiterate women drawn from jails, alleys, and saloons. Whatever, none of these so-called "nurses," whether they be Sisters of Charity, feverish patients, or female felons or drunks, had any formal training for the work.

Here and there, some practical training and medical explanations were given. For example, the New England Hospital for Women and Children in Roxbury, Massachusetts, initiated a short course in nursing in 1872. The course was the beginning of the American response to the long campaign waged by Florence Nightingale in England to improve hospital conditions and patient care. Bellevue followed the example set by Miss Nightingale, requiring nurses to wear uniforms and maintain discipline. The nursing programs offered by Bellevue, New Haven, and Massachusetts General were not yet connected to university training as they would be before the century would close. Nevertheless, these first formal schools of nursing begun in 1873 were offered only to the literate, middle class women with good backgrounds who could pass an entrance examination.

Soon thereafter, several hundred hospital-based

NURSES' CAPS

"schools" of nursing were flourishing in the United States. Unfortunately, not enough of these followed the strict standards set by Bellevue, New Haven and Massachusetts General. The women who enrolled in these schools were trained as hospital orderlies and did more cleaning up and dirty work than caring for the sick. The high quality of women in nursing was being threatened. Once again, hospital nursing began to attract that unwanted element of society that had previously permeated the hospital routine with their lack of qualification and compassion.

The downward trend in nursing qualification quickly reversed itself. Johns Hopkins Hospital of Baltimore, Maryland, founded in 1876 by wealthy business man Johns Hopkins, devised a rigid program of nursing education. Both the hospital and Johns Hopkins University and their interconnecting medical school raised the quality of admissions and instruction, thus elevating the standards necessary for a "profession" of nursing.

The Johns Hopkins nursing education program became so successful that it led to the separation by law of those who received extensive and formal nursing education—the registered or graduate nurse—from those who did not, or at best received substantially less training—the practical nurse. The registered nurse, also sometimes called the "professional" nurse, was permitted, for example, to perform some medical functions like assisting a surgeon during an operation, or injecting a needle into a patient's arm. The practical nurse, on the other hand, did not perform such medical chores but rather did those tasks like making beds or bathing patients—tasks that would relieve the graduate nurse for more important medical duties. In time, the professional education of a nurse would lead to a university degree. The training of a practical nurse which did not require such extensive education did not lead to a degree.

Toward the end of the century, more hospitals would be established in the still fast growing United States. Two of these would become extraordinary and noteworthy, but for different reasons.

In 1889, the Sisters of St. Frances, a nursing order, and more completely known as the Sisters of St. Frances of the Congregation of Our Lady of Lourdes, founded St. Mary's Hospital in Rochester, Minnesota, an area packed with Norwegian immigrants. In addition to the sisters who ran the hospital and provided for the care of the patients, there were three doctors: the brothers William James Mayo and Charles Horace Mayo and their father, William Worrel Mayo. All three physicians were surgeons. Out of this, some twenty years later, would come the Mayo Clinic. William Worrell Mayo died in 1911. But his sons became two of the most famous surgeons in the world, giving the Mayo Clinic a world-wide reputation for diagnosis and surgery—the best the science of medicine could offer.

Not far away in Chicago—on the city's South Side—and not long after the first patient was examined at St. Mary's Hospital, the first American hospital devoted to the care of the black community opened its doors. That was in 1890. The hospital, Provident Hospital, was the result of the efforts of one of the first black Americans to become a physician, Daniel Hale Williams of Pennsylvania. Three years later, in 1893, Dr. Williams successfully performed the first major heart surgery in the United States. He sewed up the pericardium—the membraneous sac that surrounds the heart—of a man who had been stabbed.

DR. DANIEL HALE WILLIAMS

As the century came to an end, the hospital had secured a necessary and accepted place in the life of the nation. The discovery of anesthesia at midcentury made people less afraid to submit to an operation that could save their lives. The risk of infection in surgery had been drastically reduced by the discovery of bacteria as

THE BELLEVUE EMERGENCY WARD

the chief cause of infection. Chances of recovery in an operating room or in a hospital generally quickly improved by the standard of cleanliness—by the use of antiseptics and sterilization. Hospitals along with their more knowledgeable staffs of doctors and efficient nursing care became safer and more reliable places to go for medical help. Bellevue, for example, introduced in 1876 the idea of an emergency ward for the immediate treatment of anyone in dire need. Together with the ambu-

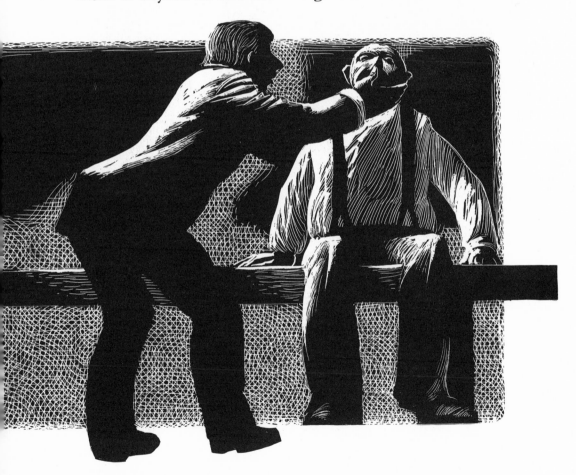

lance service, it quickened the hospital's response to public suffering—especially in accident cases.

At the beginning of the 19th century, a hospitalized patient had little chance of surviving, but by the end of the century, a patient had an excellent chance of recovery.

By 1899, much that was careless, misunderstood, and primitive in the American hospital routine was being swept away with the past. Although there was still much to be done, the practice and science of medicine and surgery and the hospitals in which these meaningful and humanitarian activities occurred, had turned the corner of ageless ignorance in a matter of fifty years, 1850-1900. The United States, in its 125 years of nationhood, had become a medically modern country.

In that last year of the century, the American Hospital Association was born. For the first time, hospitals grouped together in a common bond of interest to improve their services for the benefit of all. The American Hospital Association sought to improve the standards of health care and hospital management. From the beginning, the association tried to standardize and raise the level of quality of hospital equipment. The association, over the years, conducted meetings and conferences so that information and new management techniques could be exchanged and the latest medical publications could be discussed.

The end of the 19th century was the beginning of the modern hospital in America.

Index